This Is a Closed Book

Copyright © Jocelyn A. Keiser

All rights reserved

No part of this publication may be reproduced, distributed, or transmitted in any form or by any means, including photography, recording, or other electronic, or mechanical methods, without the prior written permission of the publisher, except in the case of brief quotations embodied in critical reviews and certain other non-commercial uses permitted by copyright law.

Certified through The Library of Congress and The United States Copyright Office

This Is a Closed Book

Jocelyn A. Keiser

Special Thanks to

My family, animals, friends, and younger self.

Introduction

This is a closed book...until now.

I have never been an open book, but my family has always wanted me to be. If you are anything like me, I would say it is a rather difficult thing to be. Yet here I am. I am going to try and be as open as possible, because only then might you begin to understand the poetry that I write in this book.

Poetry is an art. An artform I have always been drawn to write about when describing my life circumstances. However, poetry was not always my go to read. Why? Because it is interpreted many ways; it was easier to write than read. My hope is that you understand my poetry in your own way.

My mental health growing up was not the greatest. You will see that in my poetry. I wrote about my hardships, mostly, because that was one form of allowing me to get it out of my head. I'd start hearing the words in my mind and they would flow onto the paper, sometimes like vomit, all sporadic like. We all have our hardships, I just wrote about mine and I hope you find solitude and clarity within yourself through my poetry, but if not, I just confused the heck out of you.

My Life In a (Not so Much) Nutshell

As I sit here on my porch with my four dogs, the fifth one out on the acreage somewhere, the cat under our barbeque pit, and the chickens roosting in their coop, I have all the intention to start telling you about me. I just do not know where to begin.

As I have said, it is hard for me to open up, but I believe it will help my mind and soul in the long run. I have all these phrases and random thoughts that run through my mind all day and then I sit in front of this computer and nothing. Do you ever feel that way too? I need a tape recorder that sits inside my mind because I do not say these things aloud, they run on a loop in my subconscious.

I must break my life up into segments. I have a habit of overthinking everything and then I am overwhelmed, and I shut down. The fact that I am sitting here attempting to write this book is a huge step, but it will be a long process. If I break my life circumstances into some categories, it will be easier for me to write as openly as possible, and my poetry will fit in for the most part. So, without further ado, I will start with my younger years and family.

My Younger Years and Family

Until I was ten years old, I grew up in a family of five. Mom, Dad, two older sisters (one half). I was a loner whose best friend was my dog, Smokie, from my birth until a few days short of my sixteenth. Bless my parents for if they ever do read this, they may not like all that I have to say, but it is how I felt and has made me who I am today. As a child I do not remember outwardly shows of affection from any of my family. No hugs, no kisses, no I love you. There was trauma and pain on the inside of that family growing up, but not if you looked from the outside.

I was a loner. That is why I went through so many friends as years passed. I'd ask myself what the hell is wrong with me? I cannot keep any friends, but felt better alone anyhow, but also craved to have close friends forever. I did not get close relationships growing up, that is the problem. My closest relationship was with Smokie. We did everything together, he would walk with my mom and I to and from school down the road, we'd play endless hours of the day. I loved him so much and I lived in complete isolation from the outside world. My parents sheltered us, so I never understood that bad things happen.

Not until December 27th, 2010, when Smokie passed away on our kitchen floor. Two days after Christmas and only thirteen days before I turned sixteen. The night before he died my sister was over and we were watching a movie. Smokie was up and down and moving around because he was almost eighteen and it was hard for him to be comfortable laying down. Now that I look back on that night my sister said that he knew it was his time, he had kissed my knee and looked up at me with those big brown eyes and he knew, and I should have known. I should have stayed up with him, I told myself. Because when I woke to them telling me about his body I was blamed for his death. I will always remember that and seeing him there and knowing I should have done better by him. Death does funny things to people, but only if they were truly tied to that other being.

This is how bad Smokies' death was on me. I am telling you this because I truly wanted this and believed it was the only way I would be okay. Because at the time I was no longer sane, I was lost, and I was heartbroken. He meant so much to me that I wished, and I dreamed that he would reincarnate into a guy; a guy that was in all forms him and would be mine forever. But it never happened and that is life; that is not how it works. So, I dreamt about him, and they were vivid dreams that at the end would swallow him whole. I started having extreme anxiety and mild depression that came with it. As I am writing this, I feel sick to my stomach because I try to keep this stuff buried. I kept his ashes in my bedroom for over a year until I was finally "able" to spread them on our land. His death hit me hard and that is all I could think about.

I wrote a lot about my anxiety and death during those years because that is what encompassed my life. I was sent to therapists because I was scaring my family with my behavior and saying I wanted to die. Now, wanting to die and wanting to kill yourself are two completely different things. I could not actually kill myself, but I hurt myself and that was close enough for them to send me to a therapist. A therapist that did not work for me. Many therapists did not work for me, but I tried, nonetheless.

I wanted to die. I was not afraid of death, rather I welcomed it. I believed from that point I would not make it past eighteen, so I had no incentive to do much with my life except the routine of what comes next. Continuing to go to school like my parents wanted and finding a job. However, when you have zero incentive, and you make it past your expiration date you fall hard and become a lost soul. Not that I was not a lost soul already. Death lurked around me all the time and there were plenty of times where I should have been gone. But when you grow up sheltered from the outside world you do not believe anything bad will ever happen to you. So, when I was almost hand in hand with death, I danced around it because I believed I would not die, since I had not already. I teased death and so death started coming to me more regularly. Regularly in the night and in my daydreams.

You see, I have an issue with zoning out. Everyone in my family knows it and cannot stand it. I zoned into my daydreams so much that I could be driving, zone out, and moments later wonder how I got from there to here. That is why I should not have escaped death as much as I did. But here I am telling you I still struggle with those issues, and I still do not fear death as I should.

These poems reflect this moment in time for me that I had on replay for years.

Anxiety Kills

Death is the lesser of two evils when you must walk this earth alone, surrounded by others. It is such a morbid, sad fact to talk about; but why since it happens to all, and all are in common. It is anxiety at its finest, taking prey on its victims. What shall it be today? Sick to the stomach, collapsing from loud noises and crowded rooms; or worried no one will ever stay with you. Sometimes you cry yourself to sleep, other times you must drug yourself. This is a sad, sickening life that people take too lightly. Anxiety is real, and it is a real killer.

11:11

It hurts to hear you cry

To watch the months, go by and by

The emotions loom 24/7

Baby, make a wish, it's 11:11

Does it still hurt to cry?

As the months go by and by?

Did your wish take effect?

Are you still stuck in the depths?

Emotions: feel them

Emotions: show them

Emotions: fight them

Emotions: shuck them

I cannot hear you cry

While the months go by and by

No more emotions 24/7

Your wish worked on 11:11

Death

Death lurks behind me

It is on every corner, every road, every path

I cannot seem to separate from its grasp

Death is coming for me

Life must be buried in my soul

Deep down inside, if I even have one

For I have not felt alive in so long

It is as if I have no soul

It is natural to feel death all around you

It is only natural then to feel life as well

How did my reality become something in between?

I will never know, will not you?

Decay

Night by Night

Day by Day

Such a terrible waste

Since we all decay

Life quickly spreads

Death slowly preys

One life we are given

We must all decay

Dead

Death preys off the living dead

My heart aches to know this truth that everyone is afraid of

But why am I not? Not afraid of death?

Because I am already dead

Dead to the world

Dead to the people

Dead to the land

Dead to the steeple

I imagine it happening at day or nightfall

Will it be peaceful, or will it be spiteful?

I am happy, yet confused to know I have made it this far

For I thought I'd be gone living between two worlds that are slightly ajar

Dead to the world

Dead to the people

Dead to the land

Dead to the steeple

The Last Thing

The last thing I will taste is the blood of my life, dying

And it is the most surreal feeling in a body that feels nothing

Summon

It was in her blood

She was under the suds

A trembling and a sliver

Of her flesh, made a quiver

No one saw it coming

She was in that room summoning

Her inner darkest demons

To come play, those were her reasons

Now the light is shining bright

In her sterile room that's tight

May all her life be a blessing

And all she summons are confessing's

Sliding

Sliding down winters snow; for it is not for the broken soul. While in the midst we see the fallen, behind the decayed forest. They were our survivors from a fort night, and now we shall be theirs.

Sliding down winters snow; there is a great longing to slow. The most suitable will make it with triumph, while the damned are slowed to a still. We cannot all be survivors, when all to survive for is ill. Then why must we survive through this life at all?

*other

*others pride

*others fear

*other, why do you make me tear?

*others doing

*others stance

*other, why are you full of ignorance?

*others fine

*others not

*other, why cannot you stop?

*others words

*others actions

*other, why only for your satisfactions?

My Adolescent Years

I wrote much of my poetry during my adolescent years. Honestly, I have written on and off my entire life up until I turned twenty-two. I quit a lot of things when I turned twenty-two, some of which I will save for later.

Many things were happening from age sixteen up to twenty-two for me. Since I lost Smokie everything had spiraled out of control. I told you how I visited with therapists, all of which did little to nothing. So, I decided around the age of sixteen or seventeen that I was going to get medication. I did this behind my parents back with the help of my sister and for that I will always be ever grateful to her, but I am sorry for the backlash we endured after. I tried different medications and like the therapists many did not work, or I got used to them. One was Zoloft, which I was on for a few years, but my dose changed a lot and I got to a certain point where the dose would not go up. Like many things you try and become accustomed to you can also become addicted to.

I am an addictive soul. I became addicted to the pills because at first, they seemed to work and so I wanted more, then they would wear off and I would need something else. The something else came in multiple forms. May I mind you for most of this time I was still on medication. I started drinking around fifteen, but I was not heavy with it until I was around nineteen. I also tried weed and cigarettes, but those were rare too, until nineteen or so.

What addictive habit I developed at sixteen and for many years after, maybe even after hitting twenty-two, was bulimia. You're thinking, well she is a young teenage girl that wants to fit in, and she must do that by losing all her weight. Boys won't like her, girls will talk about her, and she will be an outcast. Wrong! Could not be further from the truth, however I did get addicted to feeling thin too. I had issues growing up and I would bottle them up, shove them way deep down into my subconscious, and it would leak into my stomach. Little did I know at that age that your mind affects your physical body tenfold. Bottling up things makes you numb to the world. My mind and body were so numb, and I loved it. One of the best feelings is feeling nothing and bulimia was my ticket to numbness and emptiness. So maybe I would not binge in the literal sense and then purge, but my mind was so overloaded that I would break down and run for the toilet because that was the only thing that helped me. I think I did a pretty great job at keeping it from everyone or so I thought, I am not sure how my mother found out, but I did not stop just because they knew. I hid it even more. Bulimia became a part of me in a huge way and I am sure my body still suffers consequences from it, but I am twenty-seven now and I can tell you I cannot remember the last time I made myself purge (maybe a year). I also cannot tell you these things won't happen again, but I am trying.

As people caught me in my addictive ways as I was growing up, I tried new addictions (or coping mechanisms). I'd tell them I quit that one thing. But in reality, I had started something else and was still probably doing that original thing. I started smoking weed more around nineteen and not long after I started smoking cigarettes. Now I will never admit that I was an avid anything. Not an avid smoker, not an avid drinker, not an avid medication taker, but when I did these things, I mean I did them! And then I'd have an absence of these things. An absence of a week or even a few weeks in between, which I figured was "pretty" healthy. This was also the time I started having sex. Shocker! Not everyone has sex in high school. Some of us do not do it until were almost nineteen. Me. And this "addiction" only lasted a few years.

Some of these addictions, like taking medications/certain dating scenes, had me messed up. I cannot remember exactly when, but I started having night terrors and my anxiety became worse. I have literally stared death (aka demons and monsters) in the face and felt it. If you have ever had night terrors or panic attacks that are out of your control, you know what I am talking about. I hate to talk about my monsters, but they were there and sometimes they want to still show up, but I try my best to not let them. They try to show up at night for the most part because lately I have been having a hard time being alone at that time. It might be because of all the crazy media stories we hear, or the things we watch, or it might just be because I was sheltered growing up and now I am not. Either way, I am overcoming these addictions and what comes along with them and through my poetry, it has helped.

Addicted Souls

Have you ever become so routine and monochromatic? Do you recognize the face that looks back at you from white light reflections?

We are now self-diagnosing our own lives, by self-preservation, liquidation, ventilation. It has become our addiction to find what preserves us most. To become immortal, one might say to another: untouchable in all three aspects: mental, emotional, and physical.

We are a peculiar species, us humans, in that we need a cover up from who we really are. Many of us do not realize we are routine in applying addictions to ourselves. It is the same story, day in and day out: apply face, drink one more, smoke a variety. If you cannot guess already, addiction has taken over many people's lives, and it is hard to break free from.

How such an insignificant routine as cutting grass can become an addiction for someone. Consume their life every other day, and for what purpose? It will only grow again to be cut once more. That is how all addictions start. They seem insignificant at first, unknowing to the damage they will cause. And like that, day three you're hooked and so begins a roller coaster of cause and effect.

Journey

Ever wonder why humans were created as individuals? It's because we are meant to take this journey called life by ourselves, only going along the way with other human individuals until we do not need them on our journey.

Change is the utter existence of life, we ourselves change, friends change, relationships change, and family's change. And why? So that we as humans grow as individuals in life.

Take everyone that comes into your life as a lesson or a gift. If they are no longer needed for your journey, be okay with that and move along.

Because in the end, it is you against the world, and the journey never ends.

Feelings

I don't know why I am irritated right now. I cannot seem to shake it. My sister tells me to be happy, but I still feel depressed, nothing helps. Nothing!

I want a cigarette, but I have been sober for a year now. I cannot go back to that. It is hard though. Drinking makes me sick anymore; really anything does.

Why cannot I be like I used to; before I became this. I do not understand what I am going through right now. And no one will tell me, show me, explain what it is I am dealing with.

This is not who I am. How do I get rid of you? Shake you? Destroy you, so you never come back?

I always feel like I should cry, but I do not know why. But when I do cry, it feels wonderful; like a high. I miss being high. Not a worry in the world. This is what addictions do. They make false realities. But is my reality real? Who am I? Why am I here? What do I do?

That's Life

Time will change people

For better or worse

It may suck

But let it run its course

You don't know the day

When you'll see the dark

So, continue to carry on

Until you see the maker's mark

People will judge you

They will suck you dry

All's you can do

Is get so high

Drink to the problems, the promises, the lies

Put on your life's happy disguise

Don't take for granted these people that suck

Soon they will be gone, which is just your luck

Four, Three, Two, One

Four legged creatures lurk at night
Never to come play in the light
Many are black, but most are white
Four legged creatures lurk at night

Three footed species roam the fields
Always protected by their shields
Many follow suit, but most will yield
Three footed species roam the fields

Two handed life forms dance on graves
Making sure everyone behaves
Underground ceremony in the caves
Two handed life forms dance on graves

One armed beings hit the hay
Never to see the light of day
In their prisons, they will stay
One armed being hit the hay

Twenty-two and up

As I have said before, twenty-two was the age that I stopped most of the addictions or at least boiled them way down. At that age, four major things happened to me.

It had been a little over six years since Smokie's death and I was at home when my mother and brother called me down to the garage. There was a puppy in our garage, only a few months old. He had come from a backyard breeder we had later found out because our neighbor had his sister from an earlier batch. Now, we had more dogs as the years passed after Smokie, but I never really wanted a dog myself nor did I bond with the others like I should have. But things just happen when you least expect them to and for that little puppy, I am grateful. I was already going through a hard time, you know that, so he literally saved me. I named him Arlo and I still have him to this day. He is the biggest, laziest baby and I love him.

Arlo came into my life in April of 2017 right before I graduated from college in May that year. Things were looking up since I graduated and I should have been able to find a job rather easily, but life does not work that way. Did I tell you he was a godsend? Well, he was. I was still battling anxiety and coming off medication for good. It was better for my body I felt if I stopped drugging it so much. I also battled my demons and monsters tenfold at that time, so having him with me at night helped because I could reach out and feel him and wrap him up with me to feel safe. Arlo went through surgeries for luxating patella's in both his back knees, he had intervertebral disc disease (collarbone messed up), and he developed serious head tremors. Too many times I thought this is it, I am going to lose the best thing that has happened to me in a long time. I should just give up now but staring at him I could not give up on something that came to save my life. So, in return I saved his.

I did not ever want to smoke in the car with Arlo in it. That right there had me cut back on cigarettes since I did not have many other places to smoke. But what really made me quit smoking that year was my younger brother. Were about ten years apart, so he was twelve. I was leaving to go somewhere, and he came out and saw the pack of cigarettes in my side car door. I do not know if he knew that I smoked before this instance, but he was so young and innocent I felt ashamed that he had seen them. I know that he had asked me questions about them, but all I could remember was our deal. He asked me (or told me?) to quit smoking. To hear his voice say that and see the look on his face, I crumbled on the inside. I told him that there were three cigarettes left in the pack, so once I smoked all three, I would quit smoking and never buy a pack again. He agreed. To this day I have never bought nor smoked cigarettes and I am forever grateful for his younger, innocent self, pleading with me.

Is not it funny how things work out sometimes? No later than about a month after I quit smoking cigarettes for good, did I meet a guy that would be my first true relationship. It worked out because let me tell you, he hates cigarette smokers. I've said in the past that I had "relationships", but this time it was different, he was different. We knew one another in fifth grade, I invited him to a Halloween shindig at my house, he stuck up for me when all the other kids had choice words to say about my skateboard back then. Life is funny! We never ran into each other after that all through school. It did not help that I went back and forth from public to catholic school, but that beside the point. My point is, I fell in love with him, fast and hard and all clumsy like. And he fell in love with me, first might I add.

I never had someone so head over heels for me and for me to feel the same way. I am no good at relationships and I am not an open book like he was and is, so it was difficult to say the least. I honestly would have my sister help me with things to say or do because I was wrapped up in my head and addictions still that I had no idea how to do anything. At some point I had to learn how to open up to him. It was slow and sometimes an ugly process. To this day it is still hard for me to spit things out of my mouth, but they will be on a loop in my head. So, when I wanted to break it off and run, I had to tell him I have a habit of running and if I ever tried to run, I didn't mean it and to help me stay. I have tried to run from our relationship almost as long as we have been together, about a handful of times. And each time he reminded me of what I said.

It has been a great relationship, hard sometimes, but great, nonetheless. In the beginning it was all sunshine, my sister said she had never seen me so happy, not in a long time. I wrote a lot of poetry about him and what I was feeling because I was finally happy, and it reflected in my poetry.

He

And today she felt. She felt those feelings rise that were suppressed for years, all at once. And she broke with each step. But he was there to catch her before she fully fell.

She did not know what to do or how to feel anymore. He took everything she hid away and pulled it out into the light. It was all coming back to her when she was alone, but with him she felt like home.

You must understand, for she was a closed book. Let no one in and nothing out. But he began to change her. She became more herself every time she was with him.

Know that this is rare, for her to feel this way. Never in her life has she needed someone to stay. As hard as this is to write, she knows her heart might break. But to feel what she is feeling for him, writing this is not a mistake.

Ponder and Wander

Sometimes I sit and ponder

If I ever should go wander

Lands and seas unknown to me

For me, myself, and I to see

Will you come along for the ride?

Walk hand in hand by my side

Mountains and valleys waiting to explore

For you, me, and we to adore

I always sit and ponder

When I see others go wander

Someday I'd like to leave here

If you want to go with me there

Heart

Some moments my heart hurts

Other times my heart courts

The feelings come from him

They fill my heart to the rim

I have tried to skim through this life

But I have been forced to slow down

Every path, every turn has been cut with a knife

Making my life's ending less sound

Fade Away

My heart is telling me to stay

My mind is telling me to sway a different way

Why must I feel so sick

So scared of what to pick

Am I?

Feeling, am I?

For my visions distorted

It is as if

You're a drug I had snorted

Anxious, am I?

For my body's contorted

It is as if

You're a drug I had snorted

Happy, am I?

For my minds purported

It is as if

You're a drug I had snorted

With all of that said

It is probably in my head

Now let's lie down for bed

Until we are both dead

My Forever

Did I tell a lie?

I got so high

Floated up to cloud nine

And neglected the signs

I said he was the one

My knight and sun

Shining over my head

Keeping me close in bed

I will not be sorry for my feelings

Even though I did not bring on these dealings

I meant what I said

I will no longer dread

This time spent with you

And the images I knew

Of us being together

Feels right because you are my forever

Prosper

I'm sharing my life with someone...

Or going to be

How did this happen?

I did not foresee

My life is changing...

I have to be ready

I know it's scary as hell

But I have his hand that is steady

Know that he won't judge

He will help you through

Find a way to speak up

To tell him the feelings within you

You might want to cry

You might want to empty

But baby don't lose it

No matter how tempting

Because you are beautiful love

You have so much to offer

Your thoughts and livelihood matter

So, continue to prosper

My Life Now

My life now has still seen struggles, has still seen the world fall apart, and has still seen better days. I have not truly written a great piece of poetry or anything since I was twenty-two. I believed then as I do now that the pain and anger I felt growing up truly fueled my writing and way of being. It gave me so much to write about when I could not say it for myself aloud.

The poetry I have written since then has been about small things that I was/am going through or about other people and life circumstances. I have also written more poetry than there is in this book because that poetry was for other people, and I no longer have records of what I wrote.

The poetry here on out is more recent, yes, and may resonate with you, with life as we now know it.

Wilt Away

Feelings wilt away

Knowledge doesn't stay

My edges begin to fray

Have I lost the light of day?

Yes, it has been years now

Since I wrote a thought like this, how?

Numb as before and yet again

No pain, no joy, no poetry then

Baffled I may be

Lost and lonely it may seem

Stuck in my head do I foresee

No escaping for me

Have I lost the light of day?

My edges, they do fray

Knowledge it won't stay

These feelings wilt away

Tremors

His head tremors violently

It was an accident years ago

How many times does it happen silently?

When I'm not there, does it tremor ever slow

I call out to him, running and hold

His head gently while petting him slow

Saying his name and that everything's alright

Until it is over, I'm holding him tight

Night Owl

At night I lie awake

That is the time I think most straight

Or I just overthink

Overthink about what's been done and yet to come: fate

I am hyperactive and hyperaware

All my surroundings become safe and clear

At night when everyone else is asleep

I move along with my life, rocky and steep

It is the night and thoughts that come along

That scare me if I don't stay strong

One wrong move and I'm paralyzed

So, the night owl becomes my disguise

My Body

Don't tell me what I can and can't do with my body

It's not yours, not his, not theirs, not nobody's

But mine, and I will say you have no right, it's my choice

Come the day, the Lord takes you away, we will rejoice

I'm not your hobby

I'm not your property

Don't put your hands on me

Unless you are supporting me

They're my decisions first and foremost

And then his if he sticks around

But there's so much more you are taking away

And now my body, is forever bound

You can't tell me what I can and can't do with my body

It's not yours, not his, not theirs, not nobody's

You don't have the same body parts

So why do you think you have a say

You don't understand the feelings

You never had to play

This part that brought on all these dealings

My Bella

Oh my Bella, so soft, so sweet

Spotted black and white

With cookie dough treats

Was she a cow or a goat or both?

She acted and looked unlike most

Our dog, raise a glass and toast

To the wonderful years of her youth

Filled with laughter, crying, and loving

Gone so soon, eight years to be truth

One day we will meet again

And rejoice in your love/hate of everyone

Please don't forget us up over that bright sun

Your moonlight shining upon us has begun

In loving memory,

We love you, Bella

Loved Ones

Grandma and Grandpa

Mom and Dad

Both were fighters

Long lasting survivors

Started out young

Together as one

A love so deep

A life to keep

Grandma and Grandpa

Mom and Dad

You showed us the way

To grow up one day

And in life, be okay

Don't worry, forever in our hearts you'll stay

Dear Kind Reader,

I am a Missouri born poetess and creative soul. For as long as I can remember, I have loved to write poetry, short stories, lyrics, and more. Poetry has been a huge outlet for me in getting what I want to say across to people. I suffered from mental health problems growing up, so I hope that what I have said here resonates with some, if not all, of you. I truly take a passion in writing and mental health and writing here today, to you, is one of my greatest accomplishments.

I hope that you have enjoyed this reading and taken away something special from it. I plan to write more books someday, but for now you can keep up with me @jocelynkeiser18 on socials.